A Tuscan Paradise

A Tuscan Paradise

Marina Schinz

STEWART, TABORI & CHANG

New York

To Matteo

and Federico

I have found a country retreat of such delight that I would be happy to live there forever. First I discovered the garden, a perfect jewel of medium size and human scale, full of surprises and separate spaces, that captivated me with its intimacy and its beauty. This was the garden of my dreams, the kind most gardeners today would not dare to aspire to. Upon entering the house I found it no less beguiling than the outside. I was smitten by its lively decoration and by its harmony with its surroundings. House and garden suffused each other completely and a distinctive spirit made itself felt, both inside and out. The place spoke to me of the eternal pleasures of country living, of times past and present, of layers of culture, and of the labor and love its owners had invested in it. To my mind, such a place could only exist in Italy.

And indeed, this intimate abode is to be found in the Tuscan hills, under a Perugino-blue sky near the Umbrian border. There is no volcano visible in the neighborhood, let alone an active one, and thus there is not even a remote chance that this house might be buried under and preserved by ashes for a humanity 2000 years down the road. Yet I cannot help but see it as if through a telescope from centuries ahead, and it is with a historian's curiosity that I record the views and artifacts of this enchanted place. The allusion to that calamitous day in A.D. 79 when Pompeii and Herculaneum went under in such a cruel way is not entirely gratuitous for when I entered the paradise of my friends for the first time I felt that I had gone back in time. The prevailing theme at Valle Pinciole, as the place is called, is a compelling relationship between the indoors and the outdoors, which balance each other to perfection. The outside with its many graceful and well-defined green living spaces is an extension of the house, while the tastefully adorned interiors are full of references to nature. Floral patterns, landscape engravings, animal sculptures, botanical prints, and myriad other nature-related objects engage the viewer in the fantasy that he is not just in the here-and-now but transported to another realm.

This dialogue between the indoor and outdoor spaces adds to the immense charm of the place. To the visitor versed in the vernacular of architecture and design, it is also a continuation of an essential element of Italian antiquity. In Pompeii, which continues to be one of our principal sources of horticultural information about ancient Rome, the garden was not only a vital aspect of the home but it directly influenced the development of the house.

*T*he upper rosewalk is
the only place from where we can get a
summary view of the houses that form the
compound of Valle Pinciole. What we actually
see here are the roofs of the gardener's house,
Federico's house, and Matteo's house. The
plan of the entire property is shown
on the map on page 172.

*I*rises, lavender, and
semi-wild roses planted in a native habitat
of oaks flank the main footpath, which descends
in several flights of steps toward the main
entrance of the houses. Located above the
driveway, the path runs alongside the
property's western border, which is
defined by a wooded ravine.

The front of Matteo's house is densely covered by the evergreen leaves of a Bignonia capreolata, a robust climber seldom seen yet perfect for a temperate climate. Its yellow flowers suffused with dark red make their appearance in early summer and blend in well with the hue of the brick pillars.

*O*utdoor stairs to the
upper floor are a traditional feature
of old Italian farmhouses. These are
located at the southwest corner of Matteo's
house. No longer used, they present a perfect
opportunity to grow a Rosa banksiae, which
covers its whole length. The prolific blooms
appear in May, and the vigorous climber
has the inestimable advantage of
being nearly free of thorns.

*The farmer's primitive house
was somewhat gentrified by Matteo's addition
of a portico and loggia on its south facade.
But the principal aim of his restoration
was to be surrounded by nature.*

Many efforts were made to incorporate the garden within the architectural complex of the house: the indoor and semi-indoor rooms were richly decorated with frescoes of fruits and flowers, trees and birds, or cunningly enlarged by wall paintings of pergolas, temples, and other garden scenes, successfully blurring the lines between the inside and the outside. The first time I settled into a couch in one of the subtly colored rooms full of whimsical artifacts, gazing through the window at the seemingly unchanged ancient landscape, I was seized by the notion that this congenial life of comfort and luxury was probably not a latter-day invention, that many of our ancestors must have had an equally delicious time in this spot—a sentiment much at odds with the self-centered twentieth-century perception that our current quality of life is better than it ever was before.

The house of my friends is nestled on a Tuscan hillside near the foot of the Monte Cetona, a magic mountain of sorts. This region, halfway between Florence and Rome, is one of the better-kept secrets of Italy, rich in cultural heritage and associations. It is not far from the golden triangle formed by the cities of Florence, Siena, and Arezzo, an area blessed by God as its inhabitants will assure you. It is the birthplace of Dante, Petrarca, Leonardo da Vinci, Michelangelo, and Raffaello among dozens of others who have changed the way we see the world. The landscape I behold—a classical composition of wooded mountains, hilltop towns, and verdant

A Roman bust stands guard in the entrance of Matteo's house, in front of the former bread oven. Potted plants - an Italian virtue - decorating the space outside are reflected in the glass door.

pastures—possesses such visual force that I stop wondering why Tuscany has brought forth so many great painters: it must be the natural result of the inherently beautiful scenery. When looking at the countryside's patchwork of terraced vegetation, vineyards, and olive groves, I am unwittingly forced to compare it in my mind to the backgrounds in Florentine paintings, concluding that this eternal landscape has remained basically unchanged.

The area around the Monte Cetona is particularly full of legend and history dating back further than the Renaissance or even Roman days. We are in the middle of Etruria, the Etruscan federation of twelve sovereign city-states of which nearby Chiusi was one. Thanks to the fertile land of the plain and the many streams and rivers rising in the Apennines, this southern part of Etruria had a healthy agrarian economy. It produced olive oil and wine 2,500 years before Laudemium oil and Brunello di Montalcino became prized export commodities and hit the palate of the international diner. (In fact it was the Etruscans, though not necessarily those of this region, who taught the Gauls how to make wine.) Rumor of a more mystical nature has it that the Etruscan King Porsenna of Chiusi, who attacked Rome in the sixth century B.C., is buried somewhere on the Monte Cetona and popular belief has of course endowed his tomb with a large gold treasure. Another of the region's desirable elements of increasing value are the many sources of mineral waters and

The glassed-in verandah is
pervaded by nature as well as by Italy's
classical past. A casual collection of
Roman and Etruscan vases, a female
bust, and a pair of votives in the shape
of feet are displayed on an iron
table with a majolica top.

hot springs with such melodious names as Acqua Santa, Acqua Sant'Elena, Acqua Fucoli, and Acqua Sillene. They purportedly exercise their healing powers on liver, gallbladder, and kidneys, and whatever other organs might be stressed from too much wine and olive oil.

The mystery surrounding the Etruscans stems from the fact that although they left evidence of a civilization rich in art, there is virtually no trace of a body of literature. We can decipher the characters used in their burial inscriptions, but the meaning nevertheless remains obscure. What is clear though from the many archeological finds is that Etruscans loved every kind of luxury from jewelry and personal adornment to precious objects and exquisite furniture. The excellence of their crafts is unrivaled; their goldwares, ceramics, paintings, and sculpture are of a rare sophistication, sometimes wrought by techniques that have not been explained or duplicated since. That there is a similar sense of pleasure and beauty in the house of my friends makes me speculate anew that this sense of well-being is not merely a personal feeling, but an endemic feature or a collective memory—a theory likely to be challenged no sooner than it is uttered, which is why I am forced to play my last card, a trump of course: Neanderthal man settled here, attracted to the gracious living in the natural caves nearby. Let me remind the reader that the Paleolithic form of *Homo sapiens* was by no means some insensitive and phlegmatic ape, but an astute observer of living conditions with a keen nose for attractive habitats, roaming around plenty in search of the perfect place, with the added advantage of having the pick of the lot. It is this search for an ideal location that brought him to the palatial caves within the Cetona mountain where he pitched his tents, so to speak, leading a bucolic life in this corner of the world which I therefore feel justified in calling the cradle of civilization.

*A little Bucchero jug
(Etruscan, sixth century B.C.) sits
on a fine, wooden marquetry table crafted
in Naples during the nineteenth century, while
the miniature box with its Greek figures is a
twentieth-century souvenir made of papier-
mâché. The flowers also span the ages: It took
several centuries of plant collecting before the
delicate blossoms of* Philadelphus coronarius,
Carpenteria californica, *and* Oenothera
acaulis *could be assembled in a small vase.
Whether or not we are aware of it, we are
ensconced in layers of history, a bit more
palpably so in my friends'
house than elsewhere.*

*T*he frescoed walls lend a distinctly
Pompeian feeling to the verandah, which
doubles as a conservatory or jardin d'hiver, for
it is in here that some tender plants spend their
winter. A carved wooden table serves as
a pedestal for a group of pelargoniums
which are tropical plants needing
mild winter conditions.

*T*he interesting markings and velvety texture of the leaves of 'Mrs. Quilter',
a so-called zonal or horseshoe geranium (left), explain why these plants are not only
grown for their flowers. On the right is a detail of another tropical plant housed
on the verandah, a calamondin, which is an ornamental type of orange tree
with small fruit that stay on the plant for a long time.

Acanthus mollis is grown for its attractive green leaves as much as for its unusual flowers. These grow on spikes and are white with purplish spine-tipped bracts. The unfurling leaves of this classical plant inspired the Greek architect Callimachus to the design of the capitals of the columns for the temple in Corinth.

History has left many strata of residue, and culture has developed much like the flavor of a slowly cooked broth (*bouillon de culture*) which after a week's casual attention and the continuous addition of ingredients becomes a rich stock of considerable depth. Unfortunately, many of the houses and gardens one encounters these days are made without refinement or an awareness of their cultural context and must needs be compared to a plain cup of soup concocted from a store-bought cube. Not so this one, which radiates a felicitous equilibrium between man and nature. It is neither a contrived recreation nor a modern adaptation of a past or foreign style, nor is it an architect's willful and deliberately eccentric projection. Its idyllic character is owed to its spontaneous evolution, which took place in pleasing response to its surroundings. There are no jarring effects, no abrupt changes, no horticultural horrors or inappropriate materials—it is an unpretentious, a happy and harmonious place.

Blue flowers gathered in May cover a wide range of plants from the wild and self-sufficient to the delicate and pampered. Shown here are, in order of size, the blossoms of iris, Abutilon 'Violetta', wisteria, a wild lady orchid, lilac, Ceanothus impressus, viola, vinca and Phlox divaricata.

*M*atteo's love of the countryside was quickly rekindled once he acquired a weekend

place, but it took several years before he became a hands-on gardener.

*V*alle Pinciole (which is Tuscan dialect for "Medlar Valley") is essentially a hillside garden; its heart is formed by a courtyard and two houses that are located halfway down the hill. This propitious site closely corresponds to what Leon Battista Alberti, the fifteenth-century Florentine architect and scholar, had in mind when he described the ideal setting for a country place: it should be a sloping site, open to sunshine and cooling breezes, providing different prospects and unexpected vistas—features often encountered in the Italian countryside. The advantages gained from a hilly, irregular site are considerable, though when faced with a steep, unplanted slope it is admittedly difficult for a pair of inexperienced eyes to envision the green architecture and intricate network of paths and hedges that could be built and transform the ground into a garden. A hillside garden, when skillfully designed, is never boring; the fact that it cannot be seen at one glance amplifies its actual space and adds to its richness. It took me several visits to Valle Pinciole before I could put all the pieces together and figure out its overall plan, for as one wanders downhill—a few steps here, a gradual descent there, a turn to the left or a little jog to the right—all the while being sidetracked by various amusing discoveries, one is likely to lose one's bearings. Losing one's self, both literally and figuratively, is one of the goals of garden art, and sometimes the very purpose of its design.

The property of my friends is located on a fairly steep slope. Its central axis, if it were delineated, would run northeast to southwest. The land, some ten or eleven acres in all, was gradually acquired in different parcels and surrounds the nuclear area on three sides. This thoroughly cultivated garden area is roughly the shape of a sheepskin, its narrow side being near the top of the hill and occasionally widening and contracting as one strolls down from one terrace to the next, six or seven terraces in all, until the terrain gives way below the last one to a sloping field, planted with hazelnut bushes in a disciplined orchard pattern; its geometric rusticity strikes the perfect note for this peripheral area separating the garden above from the open farmland below. On the western side, a natural boundary is formed by the hillside dropping off sharply; the ravine's sylvan habitat of oaks, chestnuts, and medlars adds a welcome sense of

*T*he view from my friends' place
to their neighbors' rolling fields holds
year-round interest; to the gardener's eye it
is at its most inspiring in wintertime.

untamed nature and permits a modest, nearly invisible wire fence to run through the woodland to keep out the odd marauder. Scanning the ground along the trail outside when on a hike down to the bottom of the gully, I could find nothing more serious than a few spikes of a porcupine (*istriche*), whose visits to other gardens is known to have caused havoc, but who does not seem much of a threat here and probably prefers its own wilderness to the secluded Renaissance ambiance of my friends' garden.

A very different scenery is encountered eighty-three yards across the lot's eastern border, beyond which one beholds the soft contours of a rolling field displaying its changing face of wheat, corn, and pasture in step with the rhythms of agriculture. The freshly plowed surface of huge, dull-brown clumps of soil that recurs with reassuring regularity in between the rotation of crops may well be its most striking phase, leaving room to the imagination while enhancing the illusion that we live in a world that will always remain the same.

This unobstructed view of the countryside is made possible by a slight change in grade in some places and by a mere ditch separating the land from its neighbor in others. Ditches have marked borders between fields forever and must be as old as mankind itself. But even such a humble territorial boundary has had its evolution and saw its status considerably elevated when at the beginning of the eighteenth century it was given the fashionable name "haha"—a semantic apotheosis not unlike that of Moliere's Monsieur Jourdain when he discovers that the words he speaks are actually "prose." Our prosaic ditch then was somewhat deepened, widened, and equipped with a wire fence along its bottom. Its installation enabled the enlightened garden architect to dispense with all-too-visible walls and fences and to include the landscape at large in his plan, keeping the borrowed view closer at hand than ever before. At Valle Pinciole, the adjacent field makes for a grand view. Grand to us that is, for a previous generation would undoubtedly have looked upon it as "just a field." But we at the turn of another century have come to regard a simple field as something precious since small-time farming is disappearing from our sight, making us ever so vulnerable to the encroachments of human settlements with their nasty by-products of golf courses, football fields, tennis courts, and parking lots. Thus, garden history is often determined not by a new invention but by a change in perception.

Cetona, a hilltop town of Etruscan origin with a medieval tower, as seen from a new room which was especially built by Federico to display this view.

*T*rue Neapolitans never leave their
native town behind completely and usually keep
a picture of the Vesuvius in their minds
if not on their walls.

*F*ederico's bedroom is decorated with illustrations of the Bay of Naples, which were taken out of a nineteenth-century souvenir book sold to travelers. The morning espresso is consumed in equally picturesque surroundings amidst flowers, on a ceramic tray.

The surroundings of Valle Pinciole are now secured and there is contentment in the air. The last bit of property along the driveway has, after a decade's wait, finally been acquired; there is no more fretting about the vistas or lusting after the neighbor's property to keep it free of eyesores. Best of all, the view of Monte Cetona has become protected too. This stroke of luck was due, ironically, to the communist party of this area that, out of a contrarian spirit and a reflexive opposition to the ruling Christian Democrats, forced the acceptance of some Draconian building restrictions that so far have kept the views pristine and filled the hearts of the capitalist residents with joy and utter relief.

Many people would be happy with a pad just such as this one, contenting themselves with the surrounding landscape and foregoing the labor a proper garden would require. Yet for some of us, the desire to communicate with nature in a more intimate way is stronger than all other considerations. Often it is not even a conscious decision but the simple urge to respond to a subtle challenge offered by nature in the form of a thirsty young seedling or a struggling adolescent tree that puts us on the road to becoming a committed gardener.

*F*ederico is sketching out
future changes in the rose gazebo,
while Tobia faithfully follows him around.
The importance of the household's dogs is
emphasized by many canine decorations
such as the framed print from an
old encyclopedia at left.

*Gardens are stage sets of sorts
as demonstrated by the rose pergola (and
gazebo) when it puts on its best show in May.
It is richly covered by 'May Queen' roses,
while a series of rectangular beds underneath
it are planted with irises, carnations, and
penstemons to underscore the roses'
star performance.*

I would not want the reader to get the impression that the owners of this delectable spot are two recluses who are acting out some nostalgic horticultural romance. Both Matteo Spinola and Federico Forquet are worldly men seeking the calm and rewards of their country home after a week's pressured work in the noise and bustle of Rome, where they live separate lives. Both have professions that require a healthy amount of travel and of socializing. The house in Cetona is where they meet and relax.

Matteo is an articulate and perceptive man, courtly, sensitive, and witty, with that particularly Italian ability to poke fun at himself. At one of my first visits to Valle Pinciole, I found him on his belly carefully scooping up buckets of rainwater that had accumulated on the swimming-pool cover and had subsequently become host to a colony of frog eggs that had begun to hatch. He laboriously carried bucket after bucket to a little pond near the lower end of the property (the existence of which had played a decisive part in the original purchase of the property) so that the tadpoles could reach maturity. A good Samaritan of the animal world must be an oddity in a Latin country and Matteo has done many a good deed: the provenance of his dogs is usually the pound if not the street itself. The latest arrival to this peaceable kingdom, a mutt of course, had been sitting near the roadside for a whole day when Matteo brought him home. He adjusted quite well, but after a few days, Giacomino, as he was baptized, ran away. When he did not return, Matteo took the car and drove without much hesitation to the spot some miles away where he had picked him up originally, and sure enough, Giaco was sitting in the very same spot, delighted to be rescued again. Matteo is known to be a dependable man.

Born the son of landowners in Carpi, near Modena, his childhood was spent in the Emilia, in that vast and fertile plain of the Po Valley that is the breadbasket of Italy (and its prosciutto, mortadella, and parmiggiano platter as well). After the war he moved with his grandmother and a tubercular uncle to Sondrio in the Italian Alps near the Swiss border, where he stayed until he took his final exams in 1950. Joining his parents again thereafter in Rome, he enrolled at the university in art history and archaeology and specialized in Etruscan studies, fascinated by this enigmatic people about whom so much less is known than about the Romans and the Greeks. Starved for intellectual stimulation and the *dolce vita* of Rome after years of

A bouquet of 'Pierre de Ronsard' roses
with some others of the 395 varieties of roses
grown in the garden.

*B*ehind the rose gazebo a section
is given over to a concentrated planting of
irises. They grow in beds around a Crataegus
prunifolia, *an ornamental tree that will
eventually create a more intimate space
and dispense some shade.*

seclusion in the mountains, he delved into the world of the theater and under the influence of Marcello Mastroianni, Monica Vitti, and Lina Wertmuller (who remained lifelong friends), he trained at the Accademia del Teatro.

Matteo remembers his three-year acting stint as having been great fun and a real walkover—I can still see that his clear-cut features and blue eyes must have been an undeniable asset—but the insight that the precarious life of an actor was not for him made him change his course. He became a press agent and in this capacity he set up business with two friends. Early on he lucked out in having Sophia Loren as one of his first clients. She had just returned from the United States where she had become acquainted with a new professional approach called Public Relations, and her guidance was instrumental in establishing Matteo's new career. He is still very active, lending his promotional expertise to the fields of theater, film, and television. Like other good listeners, Matteo is very discreet and does not bandy about names. When he arrives in Cetona, ready to throw himself into the garden, he usually leaves his professional world behind. Friends are welcome, probably more so in winter than in summer, as long as it is understood that he has work to do and is allowed to potter off once mealtime is over.

Federico, on the other hand, is apt to return to the country from the eternal city, or from some other European glamour spot, full of amusing anecdotes. He is the dinner guest par excellence, urbane, jovial, well informed, multi-talented, and polyglot. A landowner's son like Matteo, this vivacious Neapolitan dreamed in his youth of a career as a concert pianist. But fate had something else in mind and Federico is convinced to this day that his life would have played itself out differently had the holidays of his formative years not been spent in Ischia, for it is on that sleepy and romantic island that he assembled what he calls his cultural patrimony in the company of his friends the painters Enrico d'Assia and Leonor Fini, the musicians Hans Werner Henze and William Walton, and the poet William Auden, all of whom used to spend part of the summer there. Another visitor to Ischia was the haute couturier Balenciaga who was something of a misanthrope and who usually showed up when the season was over. At that time he was every young designer's idol. One day, the great man happened to be present while Federico and his musical friends were discussing a production of the San Carlo Opera, its stage sets and its costumes. Balenciaga noticed that the young man had a distinct flair for

$\mathcal{A}$ crosswalk a few steps down
and parallel to the rose pergola leads to the
open countryside where the garden ends. Irises,
selected to bloom simultaneously with the roses
in the gazebo, are planted in separate beds on
either side of it. The irises are, as on the
previous page, 'Bright Herald', 'Royal
Tapestry', and 'Dancer's Veil'.

*F*ederico's house as seen from the far
end of the iris walk. A laurel hedge with
an arched opening divides the long terrace into
shorter sections, which makes the space more
interesting and allows for variations in
the planting. Here at the periphery,
foxgloves have been added for a
more ephemeral effect.

Gazebos are excellent ploys in helping roses achieve a triumphant performance. Federico designed this iron trellis pavilion to support the rambling 'May Queen'.

fashion design and prompted him to sketch out some 120 dress designs based on a handful of themes. He was so impressed by Federico's talent that he offered him a job on the spot. Federico accepted, to the perplexity of his parents who had hoped their son would become the administrator of their landholdings in Puglia. Nevertheless they did not oppose his plans, and so he went to Paris where he was properly apprenticed to the master. After teaching his protégé all he could, Balenciaga pushed him into a career of his own and thus Federico returned two years later to Italy. At first he collaborated with Irene Galitzine in Rome, but in 1961 he opened his own couturier salon at number 9, Via Condotti, just below the Spanish steps, where he almost instantly became a success. Numerous albums in decorative boxes kept in the cabinets of the so-called summer room at Valle Pinciole contain the yellowing newspaper clippings and magazine articles illustrating Federico's comet-like career as one of Italy's foremost fashion designers. Captions like "dash, daring, dramatic and dynamic" accompany the bold creations of "Frederick the Great," who concerned himself with every aspect of fashion including the creation of his own fabrics. Listing the names of Federico's acquaintances at this stage of his life would burst the binding of this book; suffice it to say that his very first client at Via Condotti was Queen Victoria of Spain, followed in short order by Marella Agnelli and her cousin Allegra Caracciolo, friends who were not

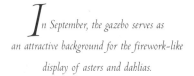

In September, the gazebo serves as an attractive background for the firework-like display of asters and dahlias.

only dashingly dressed by him but who later also became his collaborators on various projects.

The next stop on Federico's career journey was a long-term engagement in textile design at the renowned Swiss manufacturer Gustav Zumsteg in Zurich. Not only is Zumsteg known for the exquisite fabrics he produces for the world's finest fashion designers and decorators, but also for his art collection and ownership of that alluring restaurant and landmark in Zurich, the Kronenhalle. Federico's twelve years of textile design have of course left their mark throughout the house in Cetona, proving that the adornment of his personal environment must have been a strong motivation for his professional endeavors. After textile design had run its course, Federico focused his passion on interior decoration, his current profession and one that seems a natural calling for this cultured Neapolitan whose sense of decor was first awakened by the sets of the San Carlo opera house and who is thoroughly at ease with the styles and vernacular of the past in which his hometown is particularly rich. Creator of eloquent spaces and collector of unusual objects, he arranges the houses of friends, and friends of friends, and takes on assignments of more public nature such as the designing and installing of exhibitions such as the recent show on Valadier, the eighteenth-century goldsmith and jeweler, at the Villa Medici in Rome.

The last flower show of the
season is offered by blue asters and pink
dahlias. These are dependable plants, even
in less-than-perfect growing conditions, and
are definitely staging a comeback.

*I*t was actually Matteo who had found the house at Valle Pinciole some time before Federico became even vaguely interested in matters of country life. Among the incentives to acquire a place outside Rome was the impulse to provide some air and space for his dogs. Predictably, given his sympathy for this culture, Matteo first combed through the Etruscan region of Tarquinia, Vulci, and Cerveteri near the Tyrrhenian coast. By coincidence, a photographer acquaintance was trying to sell a house he had been given in lieu of payment and brought Matteo to the Chiusi area. The house in question proved to be a disappointment, but the newly discovered neighborhood worked its potent magic. Matteo looked around further, and one rosy, cool morning, when the valley was bathed in that limpid light so particular to the Italian hills, he was shown a primitive little farmhouse in the midst of vineyards and olive groves with a view of the mountain and the village of Cetona. It was love at first sight. Since water was present—always a vital question in southern countries—a deal was made, and in 1969 Matteo bought the simple hovel with its nearby *rustico* (barn), the aforementioned puddle of water, and the seven acres that came with them.

The farmer, happy to have sold, moved away like so many other *contadini* in those years. Since land on hills is hard to farm and does not yield abundant crops, the peasant population in and around Cetona had been reduced by more than two-thirds during the last generation. A hundred or so homesteads were saved and fixed up as weekend houses. Today, farming is making a comeback, albeit in an altered form. As the myth of factory work, which—quite incomprehensibly—was such a powerful lure earlier in this century, is on the wane, some members of the younger generation are returning to the land of their forebears as builders, tilers, and electricians for whom there is an increasing demand as weekend culture spreads its roots. Returning to the family patch, they take pride again in cultivating a piece of land of their own, thus illustrating the ebb and flow of demographic change that has marked our century.

When I look at photographs of Matteo's newly acquired homestead—the so-called "before" pictures—I can hardly believe the metamorphosis that has taken place in the comparatively short span of twenty-five years. It takes a real effort to recognize the original dwelling, a modest cubic structure in that picturesque state of dilapidation that is so charming when seen in the landscape and such a daunting surprise, or even rude shock, when it suddenly becomes one's own.

*C*alm and peace are
assured in the giardino delle piante
aromatiche, *an enclosure that recalls the
medieval monastery gardens and the spirit
of St. Francis. Beyond it is another
garden room. It is devoted to white
flowers, among which a 'Kiftsgate'
rose reaches impressive heights
and blooms in May.*

*T*he herb garden, located in
the courtyard between the two houses,
is stocked with more than thirty fragrant
plants such as bronze fennel, white lavender,
Geranium macrorrhizum, Tanacetum
haradjani, *and similar select specimens.*
On the other side of the dividing
wall we see the back of
Matteo's house.

The six square beds in the middle of the herb garden are given height by alliums, clary sage, and lovage in summertime (below), while in the fall two Poncirus trifoliata trained as miniature trees show off their pretty round fruit and compensate for the disappearance of the flowers (above).

*L*ooking *from Federico's summer room toward Matteo's house we are near the herb garden (above). Seen from Matteo's house, the white garden is in the foreground, where a* Deutzia lemoinei *is in full bloom. Other white-flowering shrubs, such as* Carpenteria californica *and* Choisya ternata, *grow in the two raised borders .*

Luckily, buying a house is a love affair of sorts, with the accompanying hormonal high that somewhat inoculates the love-struck individual against a slew of unforeseen expenses and costly repairs. Matteo still gives proud and affectionate descriptions of the way the place originally looked and how the first changes were made: in 1970, the two-story house was transformed into a livable home with modern amenities. The restoration yielded a nine-by-ten-yard living room with a dining corner, a kitchen, and a miniature guest room with a shower on the ground floor, and a bathroom and two bedrooms on the upper floor. The typically rural stairs outside the house were left untouched, while the interior ladder, which connected the two stories, was replaced by a staircase. This was the original nucleus from which the house grew, organically as it were.

After the first restoration, things stayed put for a few years. The relationship to the house was extremely relaxed; not every weekend was spent there. But then, suddenly, things started to move, a development comparable to the behavior of certain plants, such as *Hydrangea petiolaris* or wisterias, that after an initial few years of merely being there, suddenly take off and amaze everybody with their vigor and performance. Country life had cast its spell, and even Federico, who had initially been skeptical about rural pursuits, became its willing prey. He eventually asked Matteo to cede him a piece of land along with the *rustico* so that he could have a place of his own. This open barn had served the previous owner as a storage place for tools and carts and had definite potential. As building permits were much easier to get in the seventies than they have become since, work began soon after the transfer. Old

Norma, ancient and deaf, but still smelling the flowers, dogs her master's every footstep. Corinna the crow, on the other hand, only pays occasional visits in gratitude for Matteo having saved her life.

bricks were not hard to find, for the countryside was full of abandoned barns and houses. Italy is a nation of masons; its building material has been recycled for centuries, eons before the term "recycling" was coined. There is more than one merchant of old stones and terra-cotta tiles who looks at venerable buildings teetering on the brink of collapse not with regret or concern, but in the happy anticipation of a deal to be made.

Thus began Federico's conversion. First he built a large living room that took up the whole floor of the barn, retaining the arches of the *rustico* and fitting them with French doors. Then he added a second floor that was to contain a large bedroom, a bathroom, and a tiny kitchen. Building fever is contagious; while Federico's house was being completed, Matteo all of a sudden got the urge to do another round of improvements and to enlarge his cottage by adding a new wing. This extension had to be on a slightly higher level and could not be planned as logic would have it, but had to be set off by a yard so as to allow for an olive tree that stood in the way. Ironically, the tree subsequently died in the great freeze of 1985, but thanks to the fortuitous detour it occasioned, the house gained an old-fashioned coziness one rarely finds in a modern house.

A tree peony at its
gorgeous and very brief best. Its beauty and
intense perfume make up for the short
duration of its blooms.

Luckily there is never any water shortage at my friends' place, neither inside nor out. From an unusually positioned bathroom sink in Federico's house, we overlook the courtyard. A quince tree blooms underneath the window.

*A*ll water in the garden is welcome whether it bubbles into a handsome terra-cotta

bucket mounted on a wall or whether it comes out of a plastic hose; tap water,

though, is never as beneficial to plants as real rain.

Federico has collected many little objects, such as straw cases and English boxes, for his fern room. The latter were produced by Victorian ladies whose pastime it was to apply pressed fern leaves onto wooden boxes and stencil their silhouettes.

At the same time, Matteo added an upstairs room next to the existing two bedrooms—which Americans probably would call a den given that it has a desk, a fireplace, and a television set to which everybody retreats when it is time to watch the news. On the ground floor, a few steps up from the little vestibule next to the old living room, a dining room was to occupy the main space of the new wing, while the kitchen was pushed out to the far end, with another room in-between that I refrain from calling a pantry as it contains no victuals. The French use the word "office" for the space adjacent to the kitchen where plates are stored and food is prepared. If that respectful term had spread to Anglo-Saxon countries, it might have helped to blunt some of the excesses of feminism.

The new kitchen, its door to the apple orchard almost always ajar, is small and simple, rather like a ship's galley. Robust and simple food, particularly of the leguminous kind, is prepared there. The amusing and well-informed writer Waverly Root theorizes that pulses and legumes are of Etruscan origin, and though we know relatively little about this tribe's daily habits, it is rewarding to fantasize that the lentil soups, chickpea purees, and bean dishes we savor in Tuscany are products of Etruscan ingenuity. Be this as it may, legumes were consumed extensively in antiquity; the four Roman families—Fabius, Lentulus, Piso, and Cicero—derived their names from fava beans, lentils, peas, and chick peas. Another Etruscan cultural contribution regarding basic necessities that was adopted by the Romans is the *Cloaca Maxima*, the sewer system; it still exists. To make up for this possibly uncalled-for digression, I would like to add, on a more elevated level, that the semi-circular or

*A*group of majolica plates in
the shape of leaves underline the importance
and beauty of foliage on a wall just outside
the fern room.

*S*unshine and a whiff of the
Far East fill the fern room, which is furnished
with a Tuscan stove, upholstered rattan chairs,
and some bamboo furniture. Its main theme is
established by thirty-four framed ferns, collected
by a British colonel in India. The textiles,
of course, are Federico's own.

Romanesque arch, which to us is the most typical and graceful of all Italian building elements, is also an Etruscan legacy.

To return to my friends' building progress: at some point the inspired decision was made to connect the two houses by erecting a pair of five-foot-high brick walls. Capped with roof tiles, the walls turn the two buildings into one cohesive compound and at the same time form a courtyard. This courtyard, which I referred to earlier as the heart of the garden, is as interesting a piece of garden architecture as I have seen. On account of the sloping terrain—Federico's house being about a yard above Matteo's—the courtyard has been divided into several planes; this is not a drawback but an asset, for different levels are what make garden spaces interesting and keep the eye entertained. Here, the planes have been formulated by enlarging a part of the terrace and making it jut out from the upper house, a ploy vaguely reminiscent of Mughal tradition. A wooden pergola supports a green canopy composed of grapes and roses, soon to be joined by a clematis, which has nearly reached the top.

The courtyard itself measures about eighteen by twenty-four yards. Within these parameters are six different sections and three different levels: one is determined by the gate in the garden wall that opens to the driveway on the west side, one by the French doors of the dining room on the south side, and one by the little vestibule of Matteo's house. The transitions between the sections and levels are cohesively integrated and treated with such natural grace that it seems impossible to reconstruct the exact plan from memory. Indeed, neither the two houses nor the

*N*ature's influence on decoration is apparent in this Victorian collector's cabinet. The porcelain pot on top of it is painted in trompe l'oeil wood, whereas the collage at left was made by Vittoria Grifoni from real dried berries, oak leaves, and acorns.

*T*he airy feeling of the fern room
is created by the arched opening whose sliding
glass doors recede into the wall; this makes the
courtyard outside seem like part of the interior.
Floral patterns and fern motifs provide
a further link to the garden.

garden is the product of a premeditated plan, but the result of a gradual process based on intuition, always with an ear to what nature has to say. Thus, each indoor and outdoor room has been coaxed into existence at its own pace, getting its flavor from the mood of the moment in a process that took more than twenty years.

Today, the courtyard is divided by a third brick wall that runs parallel to the two enclosing ones, slicing off a section on the east side that is about six feet wide. An opening at the northern end leads into the upper half of this narrower section, which is the herb garden or, more poetically in Italian, *il giardino delle piante aromatiche*. Its seclusion and intimacy are very much in the spirit of the medieval cloister garden, where nuns or monks tended their apothecary plots and put their knowledge of plants into the service of the sick or the lovesick of the world, wherever the need arose. Lavender, sage, and artemisias fill the air with their strong scents that are intensified by the warmth given off by the surrounding brick walls; these store up and reflect the day's heat until well after the sun has started its descent. The paths among the beds in the middle and the borders at the foot of the walls are narrow and as one strolls to the opposite opening in the wall, one inevitably brushes against the aromatic plants. Whether this is cleverly intended or the result of genuine lack of space I cannot say. At any rate, it is a perfect small garden and a case in point that one need not be rich as Croesus to have a jewel of one's own. All by itself the seventy-nine yard plot with its six central beds and surrounding borders would barely take an hour of work a week, though it is of course within the avid gardener's natural disposition to find more to do than what is strictly necessary lest the time spent with one's plants be too short. Since the French doors of the upper house's summer room open onto the herb garden, the two spaces become a small world of their own, secluded and content; here visitors are inevitably drawn not just to the plants' scents, but to their structure and habit of growth: a most enjoyable lesson in botany.

While counting the many fragrant plants in the herb garden, I was visited by a crow who displayed an uncanny interest in what I was doing. Its friendly presence reminded me that Assisi was not far away, and that Saint Francis must of course have been one of the geniuses who had a finger in this place and pie. (Later on I learned that St. Francis had founded one of his first convents outside of Assisi on the Monte Cetona in 1212 and that, under the aegis of padre Egidio, still does

The stand of bamboo in the woodland garden is not only of botanical but also sentimental interest. The original stalks were a gift from the garden of Villa Savoia, the residence of King Vittorio Emanuele III in Rome.

good works and is now a commune for rehabilitated drug users.) The crow, it turned out, had been saved by Matteo when he extracted it from the claws of two Roman cats and brought it to the country for recovery. His amicable disposition toward the surrounding fauna is further evidenced by the many little birdhouses and feeding stations sprinkled throughout the garden—though whether Italy's decimated birdlife is deserving of such an opulent collective noun as "fauna" is of course a whole other question. That the Italian dictionary renders the Italian *corvo* as both crow and raven is a further lexical confusion that makes any bird-watcher's hair stand on end.

*T*he somewhat oriental
air of the fern room is due to such objects
as the bamboo coat rack (albeit of French or
English origin), a Chinese birdcage, a Japanese
umbrella, and an Asian straw hat.

*M*uch in contrast to the monastic spirit of the herb garden is the accumulation of worldly goods within the two houses. Each room has its own delightful ambiance and identity. Distinct color schemes are achieved by the relatively simple means of painted walls with some stencil work applied, their tints not totally unrelated to the Pompeian decorations of old. The furniture everywhere is sumptuously upholstered and extremely comfortable, beckoning the visitor to settle down in this room or that and to breathe in its very special atmosphere. Wondrous objects are distributed throughout the rooms, articles full of meaning and sentiment, their selection based on a subjective sense of beauty that relies on association and memory and is devoid of that ostentation that so often typifies the collecting of valuable artifacts.

The fern room, the largest and original living room located in the old *rustico*, is the first to deserve our attention. It takes a leap of the imagination to find oneself back in the former barn, which in all likelihood was packed with wood stacks, demijohns (large wine bottles encased in straw), bales of hay, and rusty tools, for it is now a spacious, sun-drenched interior with a light terra-cotta floor and pale blue walls. Faded linen curtains flutter in typical Mediterranean style inside the open sliding doors, catching the summer breeze and keeping out the heat of the day. An antique Tuscan majolica stove sits in one corner of the room, while an assortment of attractive rattan and bamboo chairs, sofas, and tables lend it an air of exoticism without seeming out of place. The cotton textiles naturally are of Federico's own design; their subdued colors and bluish-gray floral pattern have a vaguely Japanese feeling, but maybe it is just the eloquent presence of the bamboo table nearby that is responsible for that impression. The main decorative effect, however, is provided by the thirty-four large-scale fern silhouettes displayed all around the room. Upon closer inspection they are identifiable as the pages of a nineteenth-century herbarium assembled by a British colonel in India. The ferns are enhanced by many other knickknacks lying about, all of which are adorned with motifs derived from nature: green majolica plates in the shape of leaves; collages composed of dried foliage, acorns, and berries; Chinese bird and cricket cages; small English wood boxes painted with a fern pattern also found on the splendid, many-drawered collector's chest that must have served a Victorian gentleman to keep his collection of butterflies, moths, or rocks organized. All of these objects and images set the mind dreaming about faraway places, or about the delights of the woods and meadows just outside.

An interesting piece of garden art near the entrance of Federico's house is a collection of spherical bushes, here being kept in shape by Ilvo. They are meant to look like balls that roll down the slope.

Federico's interest in nature as an influential theme in decoration preceded his involvement in horticulture by many years; most of his life he did not have a clue that he would ever dig around in the soil. Even his friendship with Lavinia Gallarati Scotti and Donato and Maria Sanminiatelli, who were all gardeners, was purely social and not based on a common love of gardening, though it did bring about the acquaintance of the renowned landscape designer Russell Page. Russell, who helped Federico arrange the terrace of his Roman apartment on the Gianicolo Hill, not only became a friend, but also the recipient of the only men's garment ever produced on the premises of Forquet's salon, a reversible blue and brown wool coat.

Russell, who was particularly fond of his Italian clients and their cordial hospitality, visited Valle Pinciole repeatedly while its garden was still in its infancy. He undoubtedly had a good time there, and generously dispensed advice as he was wont to do when staying with friends. His interest fastened itself enthusiastically to the courtyard, for which he designed a little box parterre with flowers, the kind one would consider a Russell Page signature garden in miniature. This parterre eventually became the victim of Matteo's and Federico's growing appetite; they replaced it with the herb garden that, in my eyes, was an imaginative and convincing change.

Stepping through an opening in the herb garden's south wall to another enclosure a few steps down, one realizes that the courtyard has been subdivided, and quite daringly so, for the available space was rather limited to begin with. But boldness is an essential ingredient in garden design and it was clearly applied here when this secret space was chosen to become the white garden. This theme proved to be a sagacious choice, for the blooms of the carpenteria, deutzia, magnolia, *Hydrangea quercifolia*, and other white-flowered shrubs look positively luminous against the mellowing brick walls, while an underplanting of aegopodium, Solomon's seal, and white bleeding-hearts (*Dicentra spectabilis* 'Alba'—a much more elegant-looking plant than its otherwise charming pink sibling) light up the ground of the courtyard's shady corner.

Russell Page added an undeniably professional touch to the white garden when he suggested that the shrubs grow in beds raised a foot off the ground, so as to bring some of the blossoms closer to eye level, not to speak of the improved drainage. He further proposed that the two beds be shaped to form an octagonal center through which one walks to get from the dining room to the herb garden. If fate should leave nothing but the barest remains of this garden, a future archaeologist would still be able to prove that the great Russell Page was active in this spot by drawing a parallel to the two octagonal pools at the Marchesa Gallarati Scotti's Tor San Lorenzo site, which are comparable in size and made of the same tufa stone. What Tor San Lorenzo also shares with my friends' garden is its owner's decision to keep Russell's architectural plan, but not many of his plantings. In the final analysis, Russell Page was a better landscape architect than gardener, though either he himself saw this differently, or else small plants and flowers got less important to him as he got older. Perhaps he was consciously searching for the more lasting aspects of garden-making as his life drew to a close.

In 1983, Matteo and Federico, who by that time had become avid gardeners, added a further enclosure on the northern side of the herb garden. It was declared to be the "olive-tree garden," named after its central player. Ten years later, presumably after another killing winter, the four garden walls were slyly given a roof and transformed into a room, the upper house's last—or maybe I should say "latest"—addition.

*O*riginality is ever present
at *Valle Pinoiole: this battalion of round bushes*
owes its existence to the exciting discovery that
nearly all shrubs can be topiarized. Among the
ones shown are various types of laurel, holly,
myrtle, yew, thuja, pittosporum,
and Myrsine africana.

*T*he salon d'été *in Federico's house
echoes the hues of the former garden that
used to grow on the same site. The grouping
of stone balls and round marbles samples
on the tapestry-covered table hardly
comes as a surprise.*

*T*he French door between the salon d'été and the
herb garden, seen from both directions.

That an outdoor space is converted into a room is usually the natural course of events, though there are some instances where the opposite takes place and a building cedes its place to a garden, the garden of the Frick Collection in New York being such an example. What is noteworthy about the new room is that it has retained the soul of its former self and kept its link with the outdoors in a very subtle way. For the *salon d'été*, as this summer living room is called, is a sun-filled interior echoing the grayish green and muted yellow colors of the former garden. Its walls are filled with nineteenth-century nature paintings that strike me as French, though they might be some other country's version of that century's picturesque approach to meadows, flowers, trees, and woods. Two glass doors open up to two different sides and gardens—one to the walled herb garden, and the other to the apple orchard below the rose-pergola walk. The center of the room is occupied by a table covered with a gracefully aging sixteenth-century tapestry and strewn with books and pretty things, evocative crystal and stone balls, a sculpted terra-cotta medallion portraying a landscape, a marble inlay of a sunflower, two brass letter openers in the form of lizards, all of which are dominated by a yellow ceramic tureen in the shape of a melon. Wall cabinets with paneled doors and ruffled cotton curtains house Federico's scrap books and memorabilia, and a desk, lamp table, and some other polished period pieces from his ancestral home in Naples further set the tone of this room, an example of a decorator's metamorphosis in its most amusing and sophisticated form.

A telltale observation about my friend's house is that there is no predetermined route or "flow," as architects call the direction in which one walks through a building. Since the ground-floor rooms of both houses all have at least one French door onto the garden, we always have a choice as to how we want to go to another room: whether directly, via the house's interior, or by taking a little detour outside, looking at a tree peony in bloom, or sniffing a favorite honeysuckle on the way before going back to another room inside. Weaving in and out of house and garden is the recommended path in this place, where there is never a dull moment for eyes or nose. At its heart is an approach to building that is based less on practical considerations than on a deep love of the countryside and all living things.

During the period of Federico's expansion, Matteo's house did not remain stagnant either. The *salon d'été* of the upper house found an equivalent in the

A Belgian majolica tureen in the shape of a melon (eighteenth century) among less valuable but equally charming porcelain and ceramic fruit. Man's artifice is matched by nature's intricate design: the passionflower is real.

A *neglected but unexpectedly lush corner in the garden.*

construction of the *jardin d'hiver,* which is to say a glassed-in verandah on the south side of the lower house. This room too was a phoenix rising out of the ashes of a dead olive tree. Temperate enough to accommodate some potted orange trees and other tropical plants during the winter months, it has, despite its Victorian function, a distinctly Roman or Pompeian feeling and was in part responsible for my first impression that this place had never completely lost its link to antiquity. The walls are painted in the earthy yellows and terra-cotta shades we expect from Umbria or Tuscany. A cast-iron garden table with a tiled top displays a casual yet personal collection of Roman and Etruscan jugs and vases, an attractive female bust, and some intriguing clay feet, which look as if they have just stepped out of the past. Moreover, the impulsive guest is allowed to touch and handle these tangible vestiges of a long-gone past, though their awesome fragility suggests that this be done with the utmost care and veneration. In spring, summer, and fall this semi-indoor room is airier and emptier—the pots have been moved outside—and the furnishings can get the attention they deserve.

Two fine wooden pieces in the *jardin d'hiver* are particularly remarkable. One is a little round table of suspected Eastern European origin, carved into the shape of a gnarled tree trunk with roots. On it, a group of potted geraniums make one look twice to ascertain where nature stops and artifice begins, until the oddly pungent scent of their brown-marked leaves reaches our nose and tells us that we are faced with live plants. The other extraordinary piece of furniture in the verandah is also a table, rectangular, with some amusing inlaid vignettes at the top of each leg; its splendid leaf, composed of rich wooden marquetry creating a kaleidoscopic effect,

The apple orchard to the
east of the two houses was planted years before
the actual gardens were conceived.

*S*tenciled walls adorned
with nature paintings and tree drawings
set the theme in Federico's library. Other than
books and magazines, the room houses a few
cherished pieces of furniture from his
ancestral home in Naples.

is a testimonial to the exquisite woodwork produced in Naples during the last century. It takes the bold hand of an accomplished decorator to make such a shining piece work in this rather rustic ambiance. But work it does, as the gleaming wood adds a certain warmth to the coolness of the room's other materials. On clear winter days when the sun streams into the verandah, we can easily be fooled into believing that summer is just around the corner, especially as we look out over a group of cypress trees that we associate more readily with the warmer season than with wintertime.

The cypress trees we see from the verandah were actually among Matteo's first plantings. His choice is easily understood: the dark dense shade they dispense is much valued during the hot summers, and their upright sculptural bodies add structure and character to a property, marking the territory and appropriating the site. Two other landscape issues were addressed at the outset, both having more to do with necessity than with ornament: the entranceway was formulated and edged by hedges, and the terrace in front of the house was improved. From there the main path, or cross axis, softly descends to the group of cypresses that form a circle and harbor two stone seats that are barely visible as one enters the dark interior, momentarily blinded from the bright sun outside. Paths and terrace are paved with bricks or with tufa, a soft, beige rock that is native to the region. Brick and tufa are this garden's principal building material and they ably convince the observer that natural-looking materials are a prerequisite for successful garden design. Many crimes are committed against good taste by introducing materials that have nothing to do with the place itself; sticking to local choices is usually the best plan.

Three or four years after the house and the terrace were finished, a small swimming pool was added. Sound instincts suggested that the pool not be in plain view so as not to be an eyesore during the off-season, and though it is located on the terrace below the house, it is reasonably well hidden behind hedges and a golden laurel tree that has grown by leaps and bounds. Instead of being centered below and parallel to the house, the pool is pushed eastward and juts away from the cross axis at a slight angle. Matteo modestly assures me that, like many of the seemingly brilliant solutions on this property, it was necessitated by the irregularities of the terrain.

The swimming pool is the only substantial body of water in the garden, and as a source of endless pleasure and refreshment, we should regard it as the modern

*A porcelain medallion in the library, the back of
which is signed:* nach der Natur gemalt
von Johann Quast, 1872.

*T*his oval Neapolitan terra-cotta relief was sculpted by one of the
artisans who worked on Naples' famous crèches during the eighteenth
century. It measures about eight inches wide.

A small drawing of two oaks in an embossed mat. Like many of the house's objects, this find is the result of many hours' worth of browsing in Europe's antique shops.

*F*ig and cypress trees
tolerate dry conditions and can
reach great age, which accounts
for their eloquent presence in
southern gardens.

*O*ld-fashioned copper
sulfate, a classic remedy for pests,
lends the trunk of an apple
tree the appearance of a
modern sculpture.

incarnation of the famous *giocchi d'aqua* of Italy's renaissance gardens, which provided the *bella compania* with much gaiety and a pretext to get rid of their clothes. A small brick structure in the shape of a rustic shed at the shallow end of the pool provides shade and the chance to rest on a built-in brick bench, which is rendered more comfortable by some cushions discreetly covered in terra-cotta-colored terry cloth. On the slanted roof of the pool-shed I discovered a colony of sedums, though I sense that these were added somewhat later, after true gardening passion had struck.

And gardening, that verdant passion, did strike when the moment was right. A typical symptom of middle age, it usually manifests itself after we have stormed through youth and are ready to take a more stable and contemplative course. Had Doctor Spock done for adults what he achieved for infants, he could have pinpointed the onset of horticultural engagement as accurately as he scheduled the first tooth, or predicted the possible occurrence of whooping cough or measles. This often passionate activity can get such a grip on a person that some people—for instance nongardening spouses—consider it a disease.

To my friends this intoxicating pursuit came as a total surprise. It happened quite innocently one day, when they went to the local fruit store. As is customary

Design questions such as the exact height of a hedge are debated at length. Trial and error eventually lead to success.

in Italy, at planting time the *fruttivendolo* also stocks a few little seed packets and potted plants. While looking for basil, the men chanced upon a simple *Ampelopsis* (formerly known as Boston ivy) that somehow caught their fancy. As they were rank novices at horticulture, they happily accepted the help offered by the store owner's son, who later that afternoon came round to their house to show them how to dig a hole, put in the ivy, and make it grow. Such was the humble beginning of a relationship that boomed and bloomed into full-blown addiction to gardening.

This seemingly innocent encounter was also the first step toward a major business venture, for the helpful young man was none other than Mario Margheriti, now one of the leading nurserymen in Italy. Once in business there was nothing timid about his approach; like the *Ampelopsis*, he raced up the ladder to the top, taking two or three steps at a time. Soon his enterprise reached a level that necessitated shipments from Hilliers, the sophisticated tree nursery in England, often to fill requests from his two new friends, who had developed a voracious appetite and as a result infused and inspired Mario with a drive he gratefully acknowledges as the fruit of their symbiotic friendship.

$\mathcal{F}$rom the patio near the dining
room we look out over the swimming-pool
terrace. An Anglo-Italian approach to planting
softens the contours of the terraced landscape
and creates a cohesive, idyllic view.

The bank between the main path and the swimming-pool terrace is densely planted with Mediterranean shrubs such as lavender in the midst of which self-seeded phlox ('Cetonensis') has managed to establish itself.

Garden making has to concern itself first and foremost with the lay of the land that is to receive the construction of a garden. In Tuscany, nearly all hillsides have been modified by terracing to make cultivation possible. On account of its clay content, the soil is quite compacted and the terraces hold up fairly well without the support of retaining walls as long as they are used just to grow vines and olives. But when the ground is dug up for other purposes, the possibility of landslides increases and some support has to be provided. Sometimes mere wattle supports are enough, but often a waist-high stone or brick wall is a better solution. The sensitivity my friends brought to the site is evident in their reluctance to change the terrain in a significant way. Their intervention was discreet, never violating or autocratic. Ax and spade were preferred to bulldozer whenever possible. Thus the basic division into terraces (which are not always level) of different widths remained the same as when the land was in the hands of the farmer. Nevertheless, I doubt that its former owner, the *contadino*, would recognize his place were he suddenly transported to this spot, but would rub his eyes and gape open-mouthed at the terrestrial paradise that sprang from his poor belabored soil.

Steps of various character take the visitor from each level to the next one. In the upper garden, a long flight of stairs, parallel to the driveway, is meant as the main pedestrian approach to the house. But I just as often chose the path on the other side

What makes the pool
interesting is that it juts away from the
house and the main path at an angle. Like all
elegant pools, it has a room of its own, which
is defined by the low privet hedge
at the terrace's end.

*F*ederico the magician
conjures up a new hedge. Only experience
can teach young gardeners how fast
hedges actually grow.

*S*ticks indicate the outlines of
a future box parterre in the courtyard. The
following year it already has taken on shape.
Dwarf apple trees are set out in pots to
add structure and height.

Gian Paolo, the gardener,
shears the box hedge below Matteo's house as it
was deemed too high. On the terraced slope of
the neighboring hillside, vestiges of a former
olive grove are still visible.

A sumptuous wisteria transforms the patio near the dining-room wing into a flowering haven, further adorned by potted plants.

*P*omegranate bushes are trained to form a tunnel at the entrance to the lemon garden. Fourteen lemon trees are set out on terra-cotta bases, each in a bed of lavender.

Brass letter openers in the form of lizards amidst lemons from the garden.

of the terraced garden, which is narrower and more irregularly spaced and sometimes crosses lawn and orchard on a soft incline rather than by stairs. Much to my surprise I counted fifty-two steps from the top of the property to the entrance of the main house, and exactly fifty-two steps from there to the bottom of the garden, not in a continuous flight of stairs, but in bits and pieces of just two or three steps up to twelve at a time. Later on I was informed that this was not as much of a miracle as I had thought, because the three wider terraces, on which the two houses and the swimming pool are located, are quite naturally sited in the middle of the sloping hill. Since the land above and below those main levels is steeper, those other terraces are necessarily narrower.

When the making of a proper garden became a well-defined goal, Matteo and Federico turned their attention to the terraces below the house first. The originality with which they landscaped these is a refreshing break from formal gardening, all the while retaining some links to the classical Italian garden past. The basic plan is well balanced yet asymmetric. A series of hedges and enclosures were planted in order to divide the three terraces into separate compartments, *giardini segreti*, providing the framework for different displays. Their varied treatments remind us that gardens are stage sets of sorts. Italy has produced a number of captivating theatrical spaces, "green" outdoor theaters such as those of Villa Marlia and Villa Rizzardi, but also some fantastic indoor ones. The Teatro Olimpico in Vicenza, with its three-star stage sets by Scamozzi, is particularly striking on account of its reduced scale and baroque perspectives, not entirely unlike this small-scale garden, which, were it any larger, would have only half the charm and impact.

Each terrace has a number of surprises. Below the pool terrace we find a classical Italian lemon garden treated in a very unusual way. The lemon trees are set out in their pots on terra-cotta bases, which are surrounded by lavender shrubs. This is an inspired combination, possibly due to English influence. In England, lavender is often used for the underplanting of roses. Here it produces its yearly blue spectacle even in the shade cast by the two oaks on the terrace above and provides a vivid contrast to the lemons. In wintertime, the tender trees are hauled into the adjacent shelter—"orangerie" would be too grand a word for this indoor storage space that conveniently resulted when the wisteria terrace above it was built. Hidden behind that structure is a geometric hedge posing as a maze; it can only be seen by the really curious when they lean out from the upper terrace to gaze down.

*T*he lemon garden in
July as we look toward the orangerie.
The blue of the lavender complements
the lemon yellow to perfection.

*M*any surprises await the visitor to Valle Pinciole, such as a green maze
hidden behind the orangerie. In the courtyard the maid shakes out a
blanket with a similarly geometric pattern.

Descending to the next lower terrace I am rendered speechless, for what I behold is an exquisite brick pergola, reminiscent of Italy's most famous one at Il Trebbio, and maybe even more so those of Pompeii. Alongside it two rows of German irises mingle their light blue with the muted pink of the brick. One end of the pergola is presided over by a female terra-cotta sculpture on a pedestal; her silhouette is emphasized by a dark green hedge at her back. Every detail has been worked out perfectly to enhance a basically simple scene.

East of the path that bisects this terrace, the pergola continues in double form: two more rows of columns have been added, one on either side. Miniature pomegranate bushes surround the foot of each column, and white roses ramble over the trellis on top. An ancient leaning fig tree has been allowed to remain—its presence is both moving and eloquent; many a builder or garden maker would have heartlessly sacrificed it. Stepping through an opening in the hedge opposite the terra-cotta lady, we enter another green, though still fairly empty, space called the "Acacia garden" on account of a handful of *Robinia pseudoacacias* that were planted to provide shade and secure the terrain. Matteo still refers to it as *dai polli*, which means "down near the chickens," for this is where the farmer kept his fowl. I cannot think of a better example to illustrate the meaning of a palimpsest in the garden: a new layer of history added by each generation, not on parchment but on earth.

A last set of stairs with an iron railing leads from the brick pergola to the garden's lowest level which is furnished with two rows of crabapple trees, each rising out of its own square bed planted with violets. The trees are beautifully shaped with straight stems and full crowns. Clusters of red fruit, which appear in the fall, stay on the tree for a long time, adding color to the somber winter landscape. It is not implausible that Pliny's garden looked somewhat like this—he did after all have a bed of violets. Roman gardens were full of hedges, topiary, and symmetrical rows of trees, and as I peek out over the edge, I wonder if there might be another terrace, perchance with Pliny's name cut in box. But alas, there is nothing else down there other than the hazelnut bushes concluding the garden, a sight that spells "the end" as in a movie one had hoped would go on forever.

*T*he lowest two terraces of the
garden as seen from the platform on top of the
orangerie. It is a masterful lesson on how to
landscape a steep hillside and make the transi-
tion to the landscape beyond.

*The restrained planting of
the wider half of the pergola includes
climbing 'Iceberg' roses and miniature
pomegranate bushes.*

The narrower half of the pergola is adorned by two long beds of pale blue irises. A vigorous Rosa bracteata grows on its roof.

*U*ndoubtedly one of the glories of the
garden is this brick pergola. Its classicism is
emphasized by an allegorical figure at the end.
Here it is seen in early June.

The staircase leading from the brick pergola to the crabapple garden is flanked by formal box hedges.

Of course there are other parts to the garden. In the continuation of the crabapple garden we find a compartment that is given over to Japanese cherries—experts at carpeting the ground with their petals in the spring. Behind it is a little wood or *boschetto,* which every self-respecting Italian garden should have, because gardening in this part of the world is synonymous with shade before all else. While the paths of the lower terraces ascend toward the east, the main path or axis near the house descends in that direction; thus the terrain assumes an unevenness that greatly helps this woodland area's aspiration to semi-wilderness. A network of little paths enables the visitor to stroll in the dappled shade this way and that—a choreography sometimes much enlivened by the unforeseeable effects offered up by the tufa paving blocks, which can get diabolically slippery when wet; their porous surface invites slime and moss. Many large bushes grow here, often white flowered and intensely fragrant, especially after a spring shower. Ground covers of *Lamium* and vinca mix with other moisture-loving shade plants such as lilies of the valley, ferns, and hellebores, which have been set out in the hope of their colonizing this woodland fantasy.

At the *boschetto's* periphery near the open fields we come to a stand of bamboo—an early gift of the oldest friend of the house, the painter Enrico d'Assia, who brought a few young stalks from the Villa Savoia, the residence of King Vittorio Emanuele III. Bamboo is used extensively in Italy and is, to the horticulturally

Gian Paolo sweeping the main steps. The steep banks on either side are planted with ivy and acanthus.

astute, almost always out of context, as it cannot shed its oriental connotation and clearly remains a foreign import even after over a hundred years of residency. It is well positioned here at the property's border, where it has been joined by some *Acanthus mollis* that invaded the bamboo's vicinity. An interesting pair of consorts, as both plants have leading roles in the decorative arts. The unfurling acanthus leaves provided the motif for the capital of the Corinthian column, while bamboo, in its many guises, has been put to ample decorative and practical uses. At Valle Pinciole, though an oriental import, it is nevertheless securely anchored to this place by the bamboo furniture and some of the Japanese objects inside the house.

These then are the classical Italian features of this garden. They were the first ones to be planned and installed, and curiously are now regarded as the garden's low-maintenance areas. Since we automatically associate the staff that attended the formal gardens of France's Age d'Or (or those of the Italian Renaissance) with a cast of hundreds, it comes as a surprise to think of those lower terraces as practical and easy to care for. But the truth is that a formal garden, when it is small and when its structure is sound, does not take an insurmountable amount of work, especially when there is no grass to be weeded, watered, and cut. In terms of horticultural history, the really demanding form of gardening came in the last quarter of the nineteenth century with the advent of English flower gardening, a development whose parallel can also be traced in Matteo's and Federico's gardening career.

The main staircase leading to the
two houses is transformed into a blue dream in
July, when true lavender (Lavandula spica,
angustifolia or officinalis) proves that it does
best in poor soil. A dream plant indeed.

*H*illside gardens dictate the need for stairs. On the left is the
informal staircase that connects the upper rosewalk with the level of the gardener's
house. On the right is the entrance to the courtyard from the driveway, which is given
an entirely different treatment by its expansive landing and potted pomegranate tree.

A *set of six steps leads from the door of Matteo's hallway up to the main level of the courtyard. 'Annabelle' hydrangeas cascade down from a bed that is four feet off the ground.*

*T*he crabapple garden on the lowest
terrace is one of the delights of Valle Pinciole
as the gleaming fruit of 'Red Sentinel' make
for an unexpectedly bright display in
fall; they last well into the winter.

*S*ymmetry and order lend this
enclosed space an air of calm. Each crabapple
grows in a bed of violets. Laurel hedges form
the enclosure while two rows of irises add
an interim spectacle of blooms.

*T*he fragile blossoms of
quince trees are as decorative
as their fruit, which in Greek
mythology were known as the
apples of the Hesperides.

A second formal compartment next to the crabapple garden was provided for the spring display of Japanese cherries. 'Ukon' is on the right.

A snail explores a fragrant quince in the courtyard. The sunflower image is executed in stone intarsia.

Squeezed in between the terrace of the house and the swimming pool is another tight, little garden. A small pergola supported by four brick columns connects it to the swimming-pool lawn, while access from the upper level is achieved by a curving path with steps. The steep bank and the five raised beds in this space are densely packed with silver-leafed plants, alliums, old-fashioned roses, columbines, salvias, and some other of the soft-colored cottage-garden plants, creating the jumble that gave this compartment its nickname—it is alternatively referred to as "Giverny" or "Miss Jekyll." This pretty garden is located just below the house where the old *contadino* had his vegetable patch. (Indian figs grew here in his day and were tossed out long ago; but every once in a while they reappear, with admirable obstinacy, after more than twenty years.) With its medley of flowers, the planting of this little garden indicates a change in its owner's gardening attitude that nicely coincides with that of garden history in general. It signifies a more intense involvement not with garden architecture, but with the plants themselves.

A settee in the hallway of
Matteo's house, as could be guessed by his hat.
The framed woodcuts of birds' nests are
from an old German book.

The Jekyll garden, a densely packed compartment, is the horticultural result of several visits to England's gardens, where profusion of planting and subtle colors made an indelible impression on the two owners. Many plants dear to the cottage gardener grow here, among them alliums, phlomis, Hebe, santolina, and other Mediterranean subshrubs.

*T*he banks of this narrow garden, which is
located on the terrace below Matteo's house, are covered with
'Munstead' lavender and salvia.

A four-pillared pergola and a medley of flowers Gertrude would have
approved of: alliums, columbines, and roses among others.

Small floribunda roses tumble over a foot-high wattle fence which keeps them in check and adds a rustic note.

*I*nasmuch as flowers are concerned, I know some boors who think that if what grows in the garden does not make it onto the table or into the stomach it is well-nigh useless. Such people merely represent an attitude that prevailed for a good part of history: plants were valued above all for their function, except by a handful of poets and gardeners. They were either useful as building materials, or else were grown for their crop, whose use could be culinary or medicinal, or yield, among other products, firewood, whips for baskets, bedstraw, dyes, fragrances, poisons, and components for wreaths and garlands. Let me remind the reader that even roses, to us the epitome of beauty, were grown by the Romans largely as a utilitarian crop; their flowers were needed in great quantity at banquets and festivities, during which the fragrant petals were dropped onto the dinner guests, occasionally to such excess that a hapless diner once suffocated. I have often mused about the identity of that particular participant and decided that, had the incident occurred yesterday or today, the individual in question most likely would have been a garden writer, one of the gushy sort, who on account of a particularly sentimental disposition must have missed the moment when it was time to abandon ship.

It was the English gardeners of the late nineteenth century, particularly the age's two leading writers and garden makers, William Robinson and Gertrude Jekyll, who focused the public's attention on individual flowers and directed the spotlight

A lesson in three-tiered planting: Lespedeza cascades down from the top of the retaining wall. Roses and evening primroses grow at the foot of it, while an early-blooming type of lavender furnishes the descending bank.

toward hardy plants, subtle color schemes, and natural plantings. Both my Italian friends profess to be influenced by English gardening, and Federico, a man steeped in classicism, is an Anglophile through and through. He has visited England regularly since his twenties and attributes his Anglophilia to the cultural affinity that has existed between Naples and England for ages—a liaison much popularized by the romance of Lady Hamilton and Admiral Nelson. Of all the English gardens visited, Hidcote, designed by the enigmatic American Laurence Johnson, made the deepest impression on Matteo on account of its seeming simplicity, understated taste, and love of plants. This is where he found the profusion of planting absent from the Italian and French gardens he knew. And indeed, Hidcote's sophisticated, asymmetric plan and its tightly structured framework of walls and hedges are first-rate examples of how a space can be organized and provided with a firm, underlying structure to best show off the contents of each separate garden. Its lesson was certainly not wasted on the owners of Valle Pinciole.

When it comes to growing flowers, careful attention must be paid to soil condition and climate. Not that trees and shrubs do not have their specific requirements too, but when furnishing a garden one takes fewer risks with the specimens that will provide its bones and is likely to use the material seen and offered in the neighborhood. Flowers are a different matter, as a great deal of shopping is done by mail.

Matteo admits that he initially derived major inspiration from perusing sumptuous flower catalogs, becoming the prey of their enticing pictures and seductive captions. Ten years later, now that the garden is bursting at the seams, he is no longer looking at them.

Flower gardening is labor intensive, and it is since these prima donnas have taken center stage at Valle Pinciole that gardening has become the ruling passion and prime commitment of my friends' lives. Gone are the long travels to India, Yemen, Turkey, and other exotic destinations. Trips have to be taken in August when Italian gardens are at their absolute worst, unsightlier than in the depth of winter—though this may be beyond the imagination of gardeners from colder zones. Italy's legendary mild climate is a myth in this part of Tuscany, which seems to have everything in excess: floods, droughts, scirocco and, worst of all, the unpredictable killing winter freezes that have returned a few times in the past decades. The winter of 1985 is still deeply engraved in everybody's mind nor was December 1996 without evils.

A young gardener from Sardinia, Gian Paolo, attends the endless daily chores. He was initially trained by Ilvo, a local farmer who had diligently looked after Valle Pinciole since 1980 and who remembers that when he first came, there was only a handful of plants. Despite full-time help there is still plenty to do for Matteo and Federico who have become devoted, hands-on gardeners, and who, despite all the adversities encountered from summer droughts to winter freezes, never seem to lose their cool or enthusiasm. When I was asking for suggestions as to what the title of this book should be, Matteo unhesitatingly blurted out "Papillon," referring not to the pretty butterflies, but to the ex-convict who escaped from Devil's Island (and wrote a best-seller about it)—a perfect metaphor capturing both the slavish aspect of gardening and the pursuit of ephemeral beauty that drives us all on. Toiling away at nasty soil, struggling with ineradicable weeds and thorns, battling enemies and disease, facing failures, these are all part of the equation, yet are quickly forgotten when nature dishes out her rewards.

Irises and roses fare well in this soil and climate and several sections of the garden are devoted to these showy plants. A rose arbor and gazebo just above the upper house are the glory of the garden in May and June. The opulence and cornucopia of flowers do its owners proud and recall the famous rose gardens of the French,

*T*he silky flower of
a Papaver somniferum, *a tame cousin*
of the notorious opium poppy .

*T*he gardener's wife is tidying up a laurel arbor at the garden's end.

On the right is an apple tree covered by 'La Follette', a rose climber.

who excel not only at the cultivation of the flowers themselves, but also at the design of the supporting structures that are needed to show them to their best advantage. Bagatelle in Paris—the paragon of French rose gardens—also has a special iris garden, proving that these are the perfect companion plants to roses, flowering at the same time and tolerant of similar growing conditions. The decorative gazebo at Valle Pinciole is made of iron treillage, recalling eighteenth-century garden classicism. It fulfills the role of being a focal point as well as an interruption of the rosewalk. As is the case in the lower gardens, the terrace here is divided into two uneven halves. This recurrent pattern is a clever device, for it gives the garden its interesting rhythm, avoiding the predictability that would arise if one saw the terraces in their full lengths.

In early summer the gazebo is thickly covered with 'May Queen' roses, while underneath the arbor we find beds full of tea roses mixed with other flowers, some of which are still in an experimental phase. Veronicas, irises, penstemons, and some novel pink-flowered strawberry plants compete for every inch of space and add that exuberant touch we tend to associate with English gardens. Behind the gazebo is a smaller area that will be even more secluded when the enclosing laurel hedge at its end has matured, forming an arching doorway to the open countryside. It is given over to the cultivation of roses and irises in mauve, purple, and maroon shades, to which a few foxgloves were added recently. In the fall, this June display is replaced by an explosion of purples, pinks, and blues, produced by asters and dahlias, which are at least as floriferous as the irises and roses and moreover have the patience to wait until it is their turn to move into the limelight. The morning fogs and mists in September and October make the light particularly flattering at that time of the year. It is a beautiful but demanding garden in every respect, as all these flowers need to be pampered, nourished, sprayed, and continuously deadheaded; the latter task, an activity considered fit for ladies, is often performed by the young gardener's wife.

A second rosewalk of looser style and more informal planting has been built on the uppermost terrace, where many old-fashioned rose shrubs are enhanced by the company of the extremely free-flowering *Cistus*—usually the envy of gardeners in colder climates. Adding to the lushness are carnations and a few brilliant, probably self-seeded, poppies. A shed built with terra-cotta tiles set at an angle in traditional Tuscan style is a welcome spot for a relaxing cup of tea.

*T*he refined tone of the hand-painted
French tea set is enhanced by the presence of
'Baron Girod de L'Ain', 'Comte de
Chambord', 'Duc de Guiche',
and 'Charles de Mills'.

*T*he wooden, wisteria-covered pergola was erected in front of the Tuscan

teahouse to give maximum shade to this uppermost terrace. Roses

and Cistus thrive on both sides of the walk.

The Tuscan teahouse is built in the local style with terra-cotta tiles set at an angle to keep out sun and rain but let in a cooling breeze.

'Cardinal Hume' rose bushes are planted on the bank, which slopes away from the upper rosewalk. 'Cardinal de Richelieu' is near by, and olive trees as well as irises grow down below.

The Tuscan teahouse is in the middle of the terrace, which is a bit shorter than all the other terraces. In front of it is a wooden pergola that frames the view with white wisteria trusses. It is the only spot on the property from where we can catch a glimpse of all the houses, or rather of their roofs: the gardener's house, Federico's house, and Matteo's house, a vista accentuated by the spires of a few cypress trees planted here and there. The bank slopes steeply away from this vantage point. Old-fashioned rose shrubs in catholic colors (Cardinal Hume and Cardinal de Richelieu) planted at its edge contrast effectively with the olive trees down below, whose silvery leaves ripple while the blue irises planted beneath them sway in wavelike patterns in the wind.

Turning to the right in front of the Tuscan teahouse, we come to the upper-most corner of the actual garden area, a pivotal point, guarded by a little topiary dog. Here we have the choice of descending the main steps flanked by lavender and naturalized irises, or ascending to the driveway, whose banks are covered by wildish 'Immensee' roses. Further up still, some new projects are in the works: young gray and silver-leafed plants have been planted along the upper driveway, to one side of which a whole field of irises has been added, while on the highest plateau of the olive grove Federico had a little studio built. Further down, below the rosewalk, a meadow is being transformed into a decorative apple orchard contained by hedges of myrtle and roses. Luckily, there is no end in sight, neither visually nor in terms of my friends' horticultural enthusiasm; if things continue at this pace, it won't be long before this book requires a second volume.

A baby snail in a hellebore in February. The snail is no bigger than a small pea.

A small sampling of Matteo's mother's blankets.

T he decorative (and seasonal) displays of the outdoor flowers have their counterpart inside the house. I have often noticed particularly good needlepoint in the homes of gardeners and have come to the conclusion that needlework and gardening are related crafts. Printed fabrics too are usually given a lot of attention, and this house is of course no exception. There must be easily over a hundred patterns in the two houses, each and every one of them having been carefully selected. Needless to say, Federico is an old hand at coordinating pillows, rugs, mats, curtains, bedspreads, slipcovers, lamp shades, and all the other niceties that go into creating an ambiance. Many fabrics are from his own textile-designing past, reflecting his involvement with foliage and flowers as well as color lessons learned from nature. Perfectionism prevails on all levels, and when a new pillow does not have the right shade, it is not beyond Federico to pull off its cover and dip it in a bucketful of extra-strong tea (orange pekoe) until it reaches the desired tint, having acquired an antique look in the process to boot.

Some special friends of the household have made contributions of particular artistic merit. Among them is a beautiful collection of cottons with fruit and flower motifs created by Marella Agnelli, who under Federico's influence has become a

A fanciful watercolor by Enrico d'Assia.

practiced textile designer. Many of the watercolors on the walls are by Enrico d'Assia, who traditionally spends New Year at Valle Pinciole and each time enriches the premises with a work portraying one of the interiors, or by adding a variation on the theme of the egg. Another highlight among the furnishings is a collection of wool blankets crocheted by Matteo's mother, who was most adept at inventing patterns and combining colors of her own choice, when not presented with the coordinated wools selected by her son to match a room. Stacks of blankets are stored in a closet under the roof ready to be thrown over the beds on damp and chilly nights. They get aired out once or twice a year, when their varied bold squares or fine stripes, spread out over walls or laundry lines, make a brilliant outdoor display.

In the old days, a rhythmic pattern used to accompany the change of seasons, which in this household is still maintained by such minor events as the airing out of the blankets. Thus Matteo's main living room wears heavier fabrics in winter than in summer; these warm up the atmosphere with their yellows and reds, helped by the flames of the fireplace. In summer the curtains and slipcovers are exchanged for the lighter Marella fabrics. On warm days in the summertime the curtains are often drawn at midday.

*T*he seasonal display of fruits
and berries in the garden stands in no
way behind that of flowers. Assembled here
are Poncirus trifoliata, 'Red Sentinel'
crabapples, rosehips, medlars (known locally
as pinciole), miniature pomegranates, the
strawberry-like fruits of Arbutus
unedo, and the purple berries of
Callicarpa bodinieri.

*P*ainted and printed cherries on a
German porcelain plate (1920s) and on a
contemporary fabric by Marella Agnelli; the
real cherries are from the garden.

The dining room with its "office" at the far end.

On one particular occasion, on what might have been the hottest day of last year, there was company at Valle Pinciole. With the increasing heat of the day the guests withdrew from the garden onto the terrace, and then deeper and deeper into the house, until I found them in the middle of the afternoon in the shuttered living room, chattering away in wonderful spirits, enveloped in the dark, which made me laugh and think of the desirable cool of the Neanderthal caves.

There is another presence in the house: it is the many books in this room as well as in the hall next door, in the study upstairs, and in the little library next to the *salon d'été*. There is everything one's heart desires, from picture books to encyclopedias and novels. Every cultural aspect of Italy is covered, with a particular emphasis on Naples. There are books on travel, on other civilizations, on gardening, on theater and cinematography, on music (there are hundreds of records too, of course). Were I to choose a place of exile, I would be well served here. And for relief from too much earnestness, I could go up to Federico's library and delve into the French and American fashion and decorating magazines going back to the sixties. On rainy days, to remind myself of the world outside, I would browse through albums containing his photographs and letters from friends. A prolific record keeper, Federico has also filled many of those marbleized Italian notebooks with his unique angular writing about progress made in the garden. The first entry, dated December 30, 1979, reads "received 'Souvenir de la Malmaison' " (a rose). For the life of me, I could not dream up a more fitting opening for a garden diary.

$\mathcal{T}$he decorator's
perfectionism is visible in every
detail of this upholstered daybed
and the embroidered armchair.

A hand-painted porcelain
tureen, a porcelain dahlia, and
a Marella fabric based on an
aster design.

Detail of a watercolor by Enrico d'Assia, depicting one of the interiors of Valle Pinciole.

Giacomino above, and needlepoint pillows made to order by a friend.

$\mathcal{M}$atteo's living room is appropriately decorated with
pictures of eggs, birds' nests, and marble dogs.

The living room in its winter dress.

*The living room in its
summer gear as a breeze comes
in through the window.*

My bias for Italians makes me credit them and their Roman ancestors with a
good many things, but especially with the invention of the weekend or country
house. Since the Renaissance, the time spent away from the main home is referred
to as *villegiatura*. This term is full of delicious connotations and has its roots in the
word "villa." The villa was not simply a dwelling, but served as the administrative
center or *casa padronale* of a farm, and came with such features as cellars, storage
rooms, oil and wine presses, granaries, orchards, and so on. These farms belonged
to city dwellers with an affinity for the countryside who had invested their money
in agriculture and who came during the summer months to inspect and supervise
their domain or *fattoria*. It is in the refreshing air of these hills that urbane Tuscan
owners not only indulged in agrarian pleasures, but found the peace of mind to
devote themselves to intellectual pursuits. Thus the villa acquired the meaning of a
cultured place, of which the garden was an indispensable and integral part.

Creating a garden is undoubtedly the pursuit of pleasure in its most civilized form. That gardens should bring happiness and repose is why they are so often compared to paradise. As someone who has looked at a great many of them I am often asked which are my favorites. The answer is easy: it is those with a genuine flavor and a distinct identity of their own, reflecting their creator's temperament and passion. They must be harmonious in design and setting; if furthermore a previous presence or culture is palpable, my admiration is complete. At Valle Pinciole, I have found just such a place. It is all the rarer a find since the Arcadian charm of its surrounding countryside can hardly be taken for granted in our age and adds to the beauty of this extraordinary spot. Moreover, the garden has a worthy partner in its accompanying house. Beyond that, the house and garden of my friends are not only enchanting in themselves, but have the added distinction of being the joint creation of two different temperaments. Valle Pinciole is a dialogue between two lively, independent, and informed minds. Federico, forever the designer, notepad and pencil in hand, is the driving force behind most innovations and changes. He occasionally sees his impatience tempered by Matteo's considerations, which come from an opposite direction. Matteo is the philosopher and gardener par excellence, the protector of each plant and guardian of the status quo—the "nume tutelare," as the guardian angel of hearth and fields is sometimes called. Yet there is no discord evident, no reconciliation necessary between architect and plantsman, nor between a man of habit and an enthusiastic innovator. It is the felicitous balance achieved in this interesting exchange, the joyous partnership with nature, the casual awareness of history, or maybe simply the pleasure and delight of this idyllic place that make it, to me, nothing less than heaven on earth.

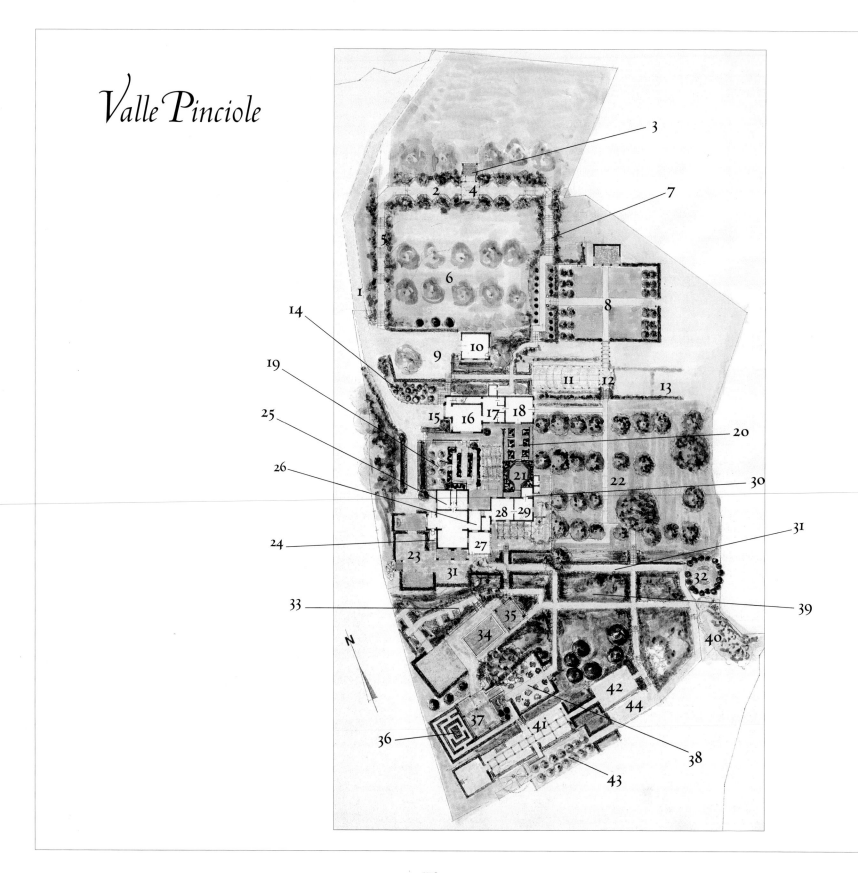

Valle Pinciole

Legend

1. Driveway
2. Upper rosewalk
3. Tuscan teahouse
4. Wooden pergola
5. Main footpath
6. Olive grove
7. Back path
8. New garden in the making
9. Parking area
10. Gardener's house and toolshed
11. Rose pergola
12. Rose gazebo
13. Iris and aster garden
14. Bed of ball-shaped bushes
15. Entrance to Federico's house
16. Fern room
17. Library
18. *Salon d'été* or summer room
19. Courtyard garden with parterre
20. Herb garden (*giardino delle piante aromatiche*)
21. White garden
22. Apple orchard
23. Entrance area of Matteo's house
24. Outside staircase
25. Guest room with bath
26. Hall
27. *Jardin d'hiver* or verandah
28. Dining room
29. Office
30. Kitchen
31. Main terrace and cross axis
32. Cypress circle
33. "Jekyll garden"
34. Swimming pool
35. Shed
36. Maze
37. Wisteria terrace (orangerie underneath)
38. Lemon garden
39. *Boschetto* or woodland garden
40. Bamboo
41. Brick pergola
42. *Dai polli*
43. Crabapple garden
44. Japanese cherry garden

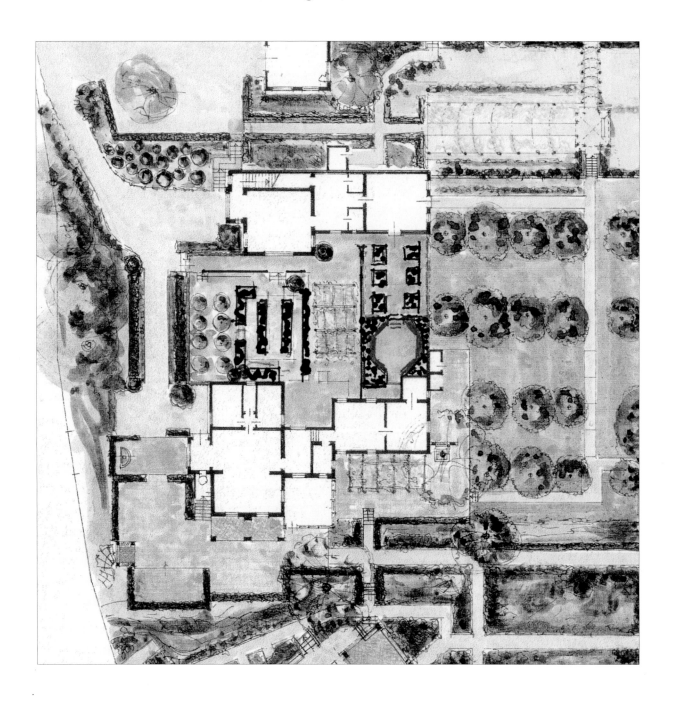

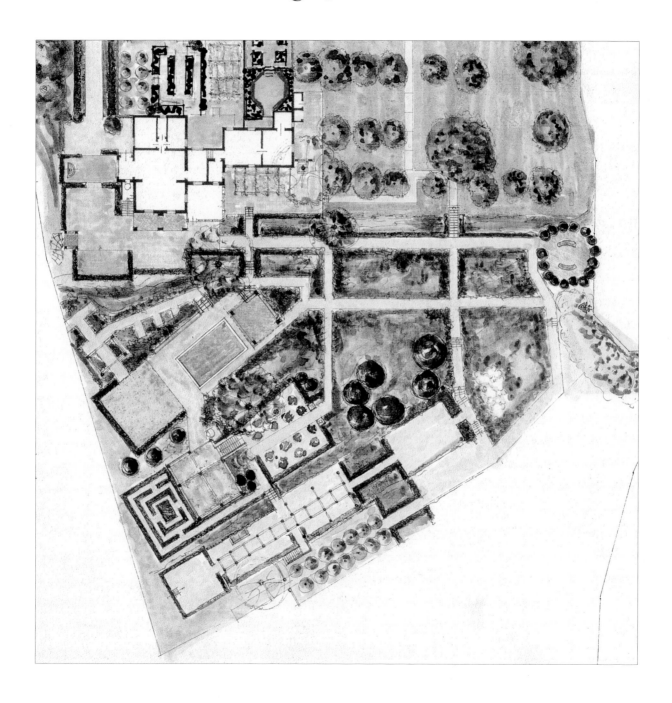

Acknowledgments

Above all I would like to thank Lena Tabori for her enthusiasm and supportive attitude, which were vital ingredients in my pursuing and completing this book. I would also like to express my thanks to my editor Erica Marcus and to my designer Melanie Random. People outside the book profession are often unaware that the making of a picture book is a collaboration and my gratitude to them both should not be underestimated. At STC I would further like to thank Amanda Freymann for her diligent supervision of the book's production and Helene DeRade-Campbell and Kim Tyner for their kind help throughout the publishing process. I would also like to cordially thank my friend Elizabeth Novick for having been such a staunch supporter of this and other projects when they were mere figments of my imagination. To Roberta Rubin my thanks for her advice when the publication date drew closer.

In Cetona I would like to thank Stefano and Rosanna Sanjust, Tommaso and Anne Dario, and Antonio d'Amico for their warm hospitality.

And last but by no means least, I would like to thank my husband Larry Rubin for his angelic patience.

Publisher: Lena Tabori
Editor: Erica Marcus
Designer: Melanie Random
Production: Amanda Freymann and Deirdre Duggan

Printer: Amilcare Pizzi S.p.A., Milan

Text and photography copyright
© 1998 Marina Schinz

Published in 1998 and distributed in the U.S. by Stewart, Tabori & Chang,
a division of U.S. Media Holdings, Inc.
115 West 18th Street, New York, NY 10011

Distributed in Canada by
General Publishing Company Ltd.
30 Lesmill Road
Don Mills, Ontario, Canada M3B 2T6

Distributed in Australia by
Peribo Pty Ltd.
58 Beaumont Road
Mount Kuring-gai, NSW 2080, Australia

Distributed in all other territories by
Grantham Book Services Ltd.
Isaac Newton Way, Alma Park Industrial Estate
Grantham, Lincolnshire, NG31 9SD, England

Library of Congress Cataloging-in-Publication Data

Schinz, Marina.
      A Tuscan paradise / Marina Schinz.
          p.   cm.
      ISBN 1-55670-686-3
      1. Gardens—Italy—Cetona. 2. Spinola, Matteo—Homes and haunts—Italy—Cetona. 3. Forquet, Federico—Homes and haunts—Italy—Cetona. 4. Gardens—Italy—Cetona—Pictorial works. 5. Spinola, Matteo—Homes and haunts—Cetona—Italy—Pictorial works. 6. Forquet, Federico—Homes and haunts—Italy—Cetona—Pictorial works. I. Title.
SB466.I82S34   1998
728.8'0945'58—dc21
                                          97-39025
                                                CIP

Printed in Italy

10 9 8 7 6 5 4 3 2 1